I0781943

TREES AND US

THE COMPLETE GUIDE TO READING, UNDERSTANDING AND APPRECIATING NATURE.

RYAN PATTERSON

Copyright © 2024 by Ryan Patterson

All rights reserved.No part of this book may be reproduced, stored in a retrieval system, or transmitted in any form or by any means, electronic, mechanical, photocopying, recording, or otherwise, without the prior written permission of the publisher.

TABLE OF CONTENTS

INTRODUCTION

Welcome Onboard dear readers, as we embark on a journey of discovering the profound connections that exist between humans and trees. This book will take you on a journey to discover the deep connections that exist between humanity and the trees that grace our planet. Whether you are an avid nature enthusiast, a casual observer, or someone looking to deepen your relationship with the natural world, this guide will help you understand and appreciate trees.

In these pages, you'll be taken through the diverse world of trees, learning about their biology, ecology, and the many ways they affect our lives. You will learn to differentiate species, understand their roles in various ecosystems, and discover the cultural and historical importance of trees in human societies. From the majestic redwoods of California to the humble oaks in your backyard, every tree has a story to tell and this book is here to help you listen.

We live in an era where the natural world faces many challenges and so many tree species face extinction due to climate change, deforestation, and urbanization. Despite these challenges, there is hope. By developing a stronger bond with trees, we can become better stewards of our planet and ensure that future generations can continue to enjoy the beauty and benefits that trees offer.

This is more than just a book; it's a call to pause, observe, and reflect. It encourages you to see trees as living, breathing entities that play an important role in our lives, rather than as mere landscape elements. With practical tips and insightful anecdotes "Trees and Us" celebrates the intricate bond between trees and humans.

Join us as we discover the wonders of the arboreal world, uncovering the secrets of trees and learning how understanding and appreciating these natural giants can lead to a more harmonious relationship with our surroundings.

CHAPTER ONE

THE STRUCTURE AND ROLE OF TREES

In botany, a tree is defined as a woody perennial plant, typically having a single stem or trunk growing to a considerable height and bearing lateral branches at some distance from the ground. But, a tree is more than just a bunch of leaves, branches, roots and trunk, rather it is a marvel of life that is part of the enormous tapestry of nature, a tree is a living thing with a narrative entwined throughout.

Beginning with a single seed buried within a nurturing soil, a tree grows from that tiny promise of life. With patience as its companion,it sends delicate roots into the ground for nourishment,sustenance and stability. Slowly it develops gradually and quietly,adding a new ring every year as a silent testament to its perseverance.

The tree gradually becomes a haven for a variety of species as it stretches above. Insects make their home within its bark, birds nest among its branches and squirrels play in its canopy. It provides shade to tired travelers and comfort to those seeking safety from the harshness of the outside world.

As the seasons change the tree experiences its own changes, it bursts forth with new life in the spring adorned with blossoms that herald the coming of warmer days ahead. Its leaves rustle in the light air and are clothed in a mantle of green during the summer. In autumn, it puts on a crimson and gold cloak as a last flourish before the winter's deep freeze.

But the tree isn't idle as even in dormancy it silently stores energy and builds strength for the upcoming spring beneath the snow covered branches in preparation for the cycle to begin anew. Thus, the story of the tree continues, an eternal cycle of growth, rebirth and endurance, a monument to the enduring power of life itself.

Trees, the quiet giants of the botanical world, are representatives of endurance, strength and resilience. Their imposing presence dominates landscapes from dense forests to urban parks providing numerous species with shelter, nourishment and also beauty. Understanding the intricate structure of trees unveils the mechanisms underlying their growth, survival and ecological importance and here are some;

The root system: This a network of hidden vital organs which lies at the foundation of the tree and is essential for anchorage, nutrient intake and water absorption. Often growing from the germination seed, the root penetrates deeply into the ground providing stability and anchoring the tree against wind and weather. Lateral roots branching out horizontally from the root spread far and wide exploring the soil for nutrients. These roots form a symbiotic relationship with the soil microbes, collecting nutrients and water in exchange for carbohydrate produced through photosynthesis.

The trunk: Rising majestically from the ground, a tree's trunk is a symbol of strength and resilience. The trunk which is covered in layers of sapwood,

Cambium, bark and heartwood acts as the main axis from which branches grow. The bark is the outermost protective layer and shields the tree from external threats such as insects, infections and physical harm. The cambium is a thin layer of actively developing cells which promote radial growth, gradually enlarging the trunk. Heartwood which is found at the center of the trunk, stores vital substances and provides structural support while sapwood which is located just beneath the bark transports water and nutrients from the roots to the leaves.

The branches: These are the outstretched arms of the tree which extend outward in a myriad of patterns offering support for leaves, flowers and fruits. Different species have different arrangements ranging from a single dominant trunk with lateral branches to multiple stems from a central point. Branching patterns influence the overall shape and profile of the tree, and reflect adaptations to environmental factors like light, wind, exposure, availability and space competition.

Leaves: These are the primary sites of photosynthesis, leaves absorb sunlight and convert it into chemical energy needed for the growth and metabolism of the tree. Their varied forms, sizes and arrangements optimize surface area for absorption of light while reducing water loss through transpiration. Leaves are equipped with specialized structures like chloroplasts, vascular bundles and stomata which enables carbon fixation, nutrient transport and effective gas exchange. Trees release oxygen into the atmosphere through the process of photosynthesis thereby purifying the air and supporting life on earth.

Reproductive Structures: Flowers the jewels of the tree announce the onset of reproduction, attracting pollinators with their vivid and vibrant colors, alluring scents and nutritious nectar. The stamens, pistils and ovules(the reproductive organs in charge of fertilization and seed production) lie within the delicate folds of the petals and sepals.

Trees showcase a remarkable variety of floral structure, which have the ability of adapting to various methods of pollination,such as wind borne dispersal or animal mediated pollination by insects, birds and mammals.

Fertilized flowers produce fruits after pollination and each fruit contains seeds enclosed in protective shells or mushy pulp. Fruits ensure the survival and propagation of tree species throughout landscapes by acting as vehicles for the dissemination of seed.

Buds: Nestled on tree branches and holds the promise of future growth, containing embryonic tissues ready to sprout new leaves, shoots or flowers.The terminal buds at the tips of the branches encourage elongation and apical dominance directing and guiding the tree's upward growth.The lateral buds lie along the sides of branches and act as reserves for new branches ensuring the development of a strong and robust canopy and makes resource distribution within the tree possible.

Vascular system:The vascular system of trees is solely responsible for the transportation of water, minerals and nutrients throughout the tree. It is made up of the xylem and phloem tissues, the xylem vessels are made up of linked cells with lignified walls which serve as channels for water uptake from the roots to the leaves. The phloem tubes is lined with living cells and facilitates the transfer of sugars and other organic compounds created during photosynthesis from source tissues to sink tissues. The xylem and phloem tissues work together to create a dynamic circulatory system that meets the tree's metabolic needs and allows for quick responses to environmental cues.

In addition to being structural marvels, trees play crucial and important roles in our lives. They are like a part of us, imagine being born in a world without trees, it will really be a stark and challenging reality to navigate.

Trees are crucial for regulating ecosystems, reducing the effects of climate change and offering other ecosystem services, as primary producers, trees capture carbon dioxide from the atmosphere, storing carbon in their biomass and mitigating the effects of global warming.Their vast root systems stabilize soils,prevent erosion and regulate water cycles thereby averting floods and safeguarding watersheds.

Trees serve as habitat and food for various organisms from the micro organisms in the soil to birds in the canopy thereby encouraging biodiversity and ecological resilience, additionally, trees improves human life by providing shade,leisure and aesthetic beauty.The importance of trees in our lives are numerous and you can't help but be impressed at the usefulness and marvel of trees.

CHAPTER 2

INSIGHTFUL RINGS: ANALYZING TREE RINGS TO DISCOVER HISTORICAL HINTS

An average human being passing by a tree may see its rings and disregard it as mere concentric circles, but what some of us don't know is that these tree rings possess an intricate narrative waiting to be deciphered.

Trees undergo a perpetual cycle of growth in the process forming annual rings within their trunks. These rings which are evidence of the passage of time have different widths which correspond to the climatic conditions that prevailed at each stage of growth. Wider and broader rings indicate prolific growth produced by flourishing conditions. Whereas adversities such as droughts or extreme temperature yield narrower rings, an evidence of the challenges and difficulties faced by the tree.

Analyzing tree rings offers a window to the past, it offers important insight into both nature and human history. Dendrochronology is the branch of science devoted to the study of tree rings,the key to deciphering the mysteries embedded within these natural archives is found in dendrochronology; dendrochronologists use painstaking inspection and ring pattern analysis to reveal the temporal tapestry concealed within tree trunks. This enables the dating of wooden artifacts, reconstruction of past climates and exploration of historical phenomena.

In dating wooden artifacts, scientists takes samples from the wooden artifacts in question, usually little cores or cross-sections are taken from the wood, after that the samples are prepared and examined under a microscope, this makes it possible for dendrochronologists to recognize and tally each individual tree ring, the sample's ring patterns are compared to existing reference chronologies.

These reference chronologies are constructed using well dated archaeological wood samples or by analyzing live trees with overlapping lifespans.When comparing the sample and reference chronologies, dendrochronologists search for patterns of wide and thin rings that match.Finding matches allows them to determine the calendar year each ring represents.

The calendar years of the sample's ring can be used to construct a new chronology specific to the tree's species and region. Finally the age of the wooden item is determined by comparing the calendar years represented by the tree rings in it to historical records or other dating techniques. By this procedure dendrochronologists can precisely date wooden objects and advance our knowledge of historical occurrences,environmental shifts and previous civilizations,isn't that wonderful!

Under dendrochronology is a fascinating field known as dendroclimatology, trees serve as a natural archive of past climate and these experts are dedicated to the art of reconstructing past climates through it.Through the analysis of tree width, density and isotopic composition, they are able to precisely deduce past climate conditions.

Dendroclimatologists in order to validate their findings calibrate their tree ring data with modern climate records,researchers establish relationships between variables related to climate and tree growth by comparing patterns of tree growth with contemporary climate data.

Once calibrated they can extend their analysis back in time, through the analysis of long lived tree species or the fusion of data from several trees and locations, scientists generate climate constructions spanning centuries to millennia.This information helps us to understand natural climate variability and provide context for current climate change trends.

In the hands of skilled dendrochronologists, tree rings are more than just growth patterns as they become windows into the past, demonstrating the interconnectivity of life on earth, like pages in a book they tell the story of cataclysmic events that have shaped landscapes and civilizations.The burned wounds created by wildfires retained in the rings of these strong survivors testify to both the fury of nature and the resilience of life itself.

Interestingly, tree rings also bear witness to volcanic eruptions as their growth patterns are marked by layers of ash and debris, a result of the volcanic eruptions.

These natural archives include exact time stamps for key volcanic events and is essential for the reconstruction of historical timelines. It's not only the forces of nature that leave their mark on these arboreal annals, human activities are also imprinted within the rings of trees.

The onset of industrialization was characterized by increased levels of air pollution and is also reflected in the structure of tree rings,indicating changes in carbon isotopes and the presence of contaminants like lead, furthermore, the rings of ancient trees provide insights into human history by charting the rise and fall of civilizations. From the removal of ancient forests to the rise of urban populations, each ring reflects humanity's impact on the natural world.

Analyzing tree rings provides a window into the past, providing a plethora of historical clues just waiting to be discovered. Experts exploring deeper into this intriguing topic will not only bring about the discovery of the mysteries of our planet's history but will also shed light on the interconnectedness of nature and human civilization. Each ring tells a tale,offering hope for a future in which our awareness of the past promotes a more sustainable and harmonious relationship with the environment.

CHAPTER 3

DECIPHERING LEAF SHAPES, SIZES AND PATTERNS

Leaves, the unsung heroes of plant life, are one of the most ubiquitous and diverse structures in the natural world with over 400,000 plant species exhibiting an amazing array of shapes, forms and patterns. From the delicate fern fronds to massive oak leaves, each leaf exemplifies nature's exquisite beauty.

Aside from their aesthetic appeal, leaves contain a lot of information waiting to be decoded. In this exciting chapter, we will delve into the captivating world of leaf forms and patterns, discovering the secrets they contain and the stories they tell.

Leaves are mostly green in color due to the presence of a compound called chlorophyll which is important for photosynthesis as it absorbs light energy from the sun. A leaf with lighter coloured or white patches or edges is called a variegated leaf.

The variety of leaf forms in nature is incredible, they may be broad and flat like those of a maple tree or elongated and slender like the needles of a pine. They can even be elaborately lobed, similar to those of an oak. Each form is perfectly adjusted to the plant's demands maximizing surface area for photosynthesis, water retention and predator defense.

One of the most distinctive leaf shapes is the heart shaped leaf,which evokes thoughts of love and affection and an example of a tree that has this type of leaf is the Eastern Redbud. It has beautiful heart shaped leaves which make it a symbol of love and romance in many cultures. In contrast, the lanceolate leaf shape, which is distinguished by its long and slender form tapering to a point, is frequently associated with plants that are adapted to dry or arid environments.

Species like the agaves and yuccas possess lanceolate leaves that help reduce water loss through transpiration, allowing them to thrive in harsh environments. Some common forms of leaves are;

Lanceolate: Long and slender with a pointed tip which can be seen on the leaves of the willow tree.

Palmate: Shaped like the palm of hand with lobes radiating from a central point which can be seen on the leaves of the maple tree.

Pinnatifid: Its prominent feature is its division into leaflets,like the leaves on an ash tree.

Spiral: Arranged in a spiral pattern and is seen on the leaves of a pine tree.

Ovate:This is egg shaped with a rounded tip,like the leaves of the oak tree.

Aside from their shapes,leaves exhibit an interesting variety of patterns,ranging from simple veins to intricate fractals.The veins act as the leaf's circulatory system, carrying water, nutrients and sugars to and from the plant's cells.

The arrangement of veins can vary greatly between species with some having a parallel pattern (as seen in grasses and lilies)and others exhibiting a reticulate or net like pattern(as seen in dicots like maples and roses).The variegation is the colorful patterns just like the white and green stripes on the leaves of the prayer plant.

The repeating patterns of shapes on the leaves are called the Tessellation, example is the hexagonal cells on the leaves of the honeycomb plant. Different leaf shapes on the same plant,like the rounded and pointed leaves on the same stem of the taro plant are called Heterophylly.

Fractals are another prominent aspect of leaf design and are mathematical patterns that exhibit self-similarity at various scales. The branching pattern of veins in many leaves follow fractal geometry, replicating the same basic structure at different magnification levels.This clever design maximizes surface area for photosynthesis while at same time minimizing the energy required for nutrient transport.

Like a cryptic code waiting to be deciphered, Leaves contain important information about the plants they are bearing. Botanist and ecologists study leaf morphology to identify and categorize plant species, revealing their evolutionary links.

Additionally, a plant's leaf shape and pattern can unveil information about its evolutionary history and ecological importance. For instance, Plants with deeply lobed leaves may have developed it as a defense mechanism against herbivores, making it impossible for them to consume large portions of the leaf surface while plants with deeply divided leaves like ferns may have evolved to thrive in low light conditions by increasing their leaf surface area.

In many communities leaves have cultural and symbolic meanings. In japan for example, the maple leaf is a symbol of beauty and elegance, while in the celtic folklore, the oak leaf is a symbol of strength. Each leaf provides a window into the inner workings of the plant and this is made possible by their ability to convey tales of adaptation,evolution and connectivity.

As we unravel the mysteries of leaf shapes and patterns,we gain a deeper a unique blend of structure and function refined over millions of years of evolution. As we keep working to understand the language of leaves,we are able to learn more about specific plant species as well as the more general ideas that underpin the diversity and adaptability of ecosystems around the world. By embracing the wisdom encoded in every leaf, we cultivate a deeper respect for the intricacy and beauty of the natural world, this inspires us to care for it for generations to come.

CHAPTER 4

ROOT REVELATIONS:UNCOVERING THE DEPTH OF ROOT SYSTEM

Despite being often hidden beneath the surface, root systems serve as the lifeline and foundation of plant life.Their importance cannot be overstated even though they might go unnoticed. Join me as we journey through this exciting chapter where we shall uncover the depths of the root systems, exploring their structure and fascinating adaptations.

Root systems are wonders of natural engineering, they are made up of a variety of structures intended to sustain plant life. At the heart of every root system lies the primary root which emerges from the seed during germination, it is from this primary root that the secondary roots extend outward, forming a complex network that permeates the soil.

A plant's roots are essential to its growth and survival because they serve a variety of functions.

Roots take up water and other nutrients from the soil to support vital processes like photosynthesis and metabolism,they protect the plant from the wind and other external factors by deeply burying it in the earth.

Additionally plants store food reserves in their root systems to assist them survive nutritional shortages and dry times. Roots grow to specific conditions which if changed can impede a plant's growth.Tree roots can grow any from two to ten feet deep. However, there are some tree roots that have been known to grow much deeper than that.

The deepest recorded penetration depth reached by a tree root is 400 feet and is achieved by a wild fig tree located in Echo caves,close to Origstads, Mpumalanga, South Africa. Another tree with a very deep root penetration is the Shepherd's tree(Boscia Albitrunca) native to the Kalahari desert and its roots are more than 230 feets deep.

As a result of the remarkable adaptations that root systems exhibit to various environmental circumstances, plants can thrive in a range of settings. In dry regions, plants can develop lengthy taproots that delve far into the earth to extract water from underground reservoirs. Conversely, plants may grow adventitious roots in soggy soils, These roots emerge from the stem or grow aerial roots and take in oxygen from the air.

There are two main types of root systems which are the taproot system and fibrous root system. Picture a single, strong root, resolute and unwavering, reaching deep into the ground like an anchor.

This primary root is called the taproot and it forms the foundation of the plant's underground structure, smaller lateral roots spread outward from it's robust base,their delicate tendrils embracing the soil. However the taproot is not merely a structural wonder but also a masterpiece of nature's engineering.

As the taproot delves into the depths of the soil,it seeks out hidden reservoirs of water and nutrients, securing the plant's sustenance even in the harshest of environments. It's vertical decline is not just a search for stability, it's a voyage of survival and a symbol of the plant's fortitude in the face of difficulty and there's much grace to this simplicity, In contrast to the spreading roots of its fibrous counterpart, it directs the plant's energy toward development and fruition, optimizing its capacity for survival.

On the other hand, the fibrous root system, unlike the taproot system which features a single dominant root extending deep into the soil, boasts an intricate web of thin, thread-like roots that extends just below the surface in a horizontal plane. For many plant species, this complex network of roots acts as both an anchor and a lifeline, providing stability in the face of environmental difficulties and aiding the absorption of water and nutrients necessary for growth and survival.

Imagine a dense carpet of roots that are entwined and interconnected dancing delicately through the dirt as they explore and provide for one another. In a symphony of biological collaboration, every rootlet stretches outward in search of moisture and minerals, forming links with the surrounding earth.

The plant's ability to draw nutrients from the soil is improved by this interconnected network which also gives the plant structural support and guarantees its vigor. Among the intriguing features of the fibrous root system is its flexibility to adapt to a variety of soil conditions.

Whether they are growing in the rich loam of a forest floor or clinging to the rocky cliffs of a mountainside, fibrous rooted plants are remarkably adaptable to a wide range of environment conditions. Because of their lateral growth, they can take advantage of even the most limited resources, accessing pockets of nutrients and moisture that would be inaccessible to plants with shallow root systems.

The fibrous root system's ability to herald life and renewal may be its most astounding feature. As these roots penetrate further into the ground, they open up pathways for water to seep through, helping to replenish groundwater supplies and halting soil erosion. Fibrous rooted plants are therefore essential to preserving the integrity and health of the ecosystems in which they live, acting as stewards of the soil and guardians of its valuable resources.

An important feature of root system is the Rhizosphere. This is a complex network made up of symbiotic connections between root systems and soil microorganisms. Beneficial microorganisms such as mycorrhizal fungi and nitrogen fixing bacteria form mutually beneficial associations with plant roots to improve the nutrient intake and general health of the plant. The resilience of ecosystems and soil fertility are enhanced by these symbiotic connections.

Also by exchanging chemical signals with one another through their roots, plants are able to respond collectively to environmental cues such as nutrient availability, pest infestations and drought stress. This phenomenon is called allelopathy and emphasizes the intelligence and connectivity of plant life.

Root systems in general play a vital role in preserving the health and function of ecosystems. By stabilizing the soil structure, they encourage soil aggregation and stop erosion. They can also help with carbon sequestration, storing carbon in the soil to lessen the effects of climate change.

In addition, root systems maintain biodiversity by giving soil creatures a place to live and food sources. But despite all this, root systems face many challenges in the modern world, such as soil degradation, pollution, and climate change.

Understanding the intricacies of root biology is essential for the creation of sustainable farming methods and the lessening of environmental degradation.

Their effects extend to every part of the natural world, from the tops of the canopy to the depths of the soil. Let us treasure and safeguard these underground heroes as they hold the keys to the resilience and vitality of our planet.

CHAPTER 5

UNCOVERING SECRETS HIDDEN IN TREE BARKS

Tree barks, the protective outer layers of trees, has been long ignored as a source of wonder and intrigue, but beyond their rough surface is a secret world just waiting to be discovered. There is a silent story of time, weathered by the elements and maintained by the hand of nature itself embedded in the complex patterns carved into the tree bark. Exploring these arboreal archives is like taking a trip through time, exploring ecology , history and the wonders of nature.

The outer bark of a tree is like our skin, it protects the inner wood from extreme temperature and environmental impact and also holds fluids keeping out pathogens such as bacteria, fungi and insects. The inner bark is called the phloem and it is within this layer the sap flows carrying the food of the tree produced in the leaves down to the branches, trunk and roots. But a tree's bark is more than just a covering of defense or carriage of food; it is a living tapestry that records the passage of time, the cycles of growth and decay,and the interactions of large and little animals, every crack, knot and scar reveals a tale of symbiotic ties developed over millennia, of adapting to changing surroundings and of resiliency in the face of misfortune.

One of the most amazing features of tree bark is its ability to retain traces of the past.The patterns on the bark act as a record of the growth and development of the tree and through them scientists can learn more about a tree life's history including its growth rate, reaction to environmental pressures and even historical disturbances like insect infestations and wildfires.

However the mysteries of a tree go far beyond the field of dendrochronology. In traditional medicine, the use of tree barks as medicine to cure various illnesses has been in existence for centuries. Tree barks possess a vast array of chemical compounds with a plethora of possible uses.

For instance the cramp bark(viburnum)was highly treasured by native Americans for its ability to prevent miscarriage, relieve period pains and prepare the womb for childbirth .This bark is valuable when there is too much tension in the body and has a particular affinity with the female reproductive system where it has a balancing effect. It can also be used to treat endometriosis and pelvic inflammatory diseases.

Rhamnus is the bitter bark of the cascara tree and is also medicinal. It is used for the relief of constipation and hemorrhoids and as a rectoanal postoperative treatment.The bark of the willow tree has been used medicinally for thousands of years to treat pain, inflammation and fever. It contains salicin and also a range of plant compounds that are known to reduce inflammation and pain. Another good example of a medicinal bark is the prunus serotina(wild cherry) and is used to treat diarrhea, indigestion, headache, bronchitis, labor pains and also acts as a cough sedative.

In addition to being medicinal, tree barks have been employed in customary ceremonies and rituals. Tree bark was used in a wide range of cultural and artistic contexts by prehistoric American societies. The ceiba tree, which was revered by the maya people of MesoAmerica, was thought to be a conduit between the heavens, earth and underworld. Its bark was decorated with elaborate carvings that represented heavenly motifs and legendary characters.

Comparably, the bark of the birch tree was highly valued for its adaptability and symbolism by native american tribes in North America,Some of these tribes were the Haudenosaunee(Iroquois)and the Anishinaabe (Ojibwe).They used it to build canoes, shelters and ceremonial objects and was decorated with elaborate patterns that represented the interdependence of all living things.

The inventiveness and craftsmanship with which people decorated tree bark evolved along with the growth and development of civilizations. In medieval Europe, the art of tree carving achieved new heights of sophistication, with finely carved effigies adorning the facades of cathedrals and castles, depicting scenes from religious texts.

The ancient oaks and beeches with their gnarled bark provided a blank canvas for the creative imaginations of medieval artisans, who used their chisels and mallets to transform the natural material into representations of human dedication and aspiration.The bark of trees still serve as a medium for artistic expression and social criticism in the present period, inspiring both artists and craftspeople.In cities around the world,street artists turn ordinary streetscapes into colorful exhibits of urban art by using the rough texture of tree bark as a canvas for their murals and tags.

But perhaps the most profound aspect of tree bark's cultural value is its power to bind us to the natural world-to remind us of our common history and connection to the web of life that supports us all. The bark of trees provides a physical link to our primordial origins in a world where steel and concrete are taking center stage. It inspires awe and respect for the age old rhythms of nature that still influence our way of life.

In conclusion,looking at a tree's beautifully patterned bark serves as a reminder of the innumerable generations that have come before us, each leaving their mark upon the earth and of our responsibility to care for the earth for future generations.

CHAPTER 6

UNDERSTANDING SYMBIOTIC RELATIONSHIPS IN THE FOREST

Walking into a forest we are surrounded by a different array of species that have evolved to coexist in a delicate balance of symbiosis. Among these, the relationships between trees and other arboreal allies like bacteria, fungus and other microorganisms are among the most important and fascinating. Understanding these symbiotic relationships can provide important insights into the complex web of life, which is essential to the survival and profitability of the forest ecosystem.

Among the most amazing examples of symbiotic relationships in the forest is the mycorrhizal network. The mycorrhizal network supports complex relationships between plants and fungus by acting as an advanced subterranean communication and resource distribution system.

Fungal hyphae start this symbiotic association by growing from plant roots and creating a massive network that permeates the earth. By acting as extensions of the plant's root system, these fungi hyphae raise the amount of surface area that is accessible for nutrient absorption.

The fungi can access food sources like micronutrient and phosphorus through this network that the roots of the plants might not be able to reach on their own. The plants give the fungi sugars and other Carbohydrates produced by photosynthesis in return for these essential nutrients. The mutualistic interaction between the two organisms is built on this reciprocal exchange.

Additionally, the mycorrhizal network makes it possible for the transfer of nutrients and resources between connected plants. Plants can share resources through the fungal network when they are in need such as during drought or nutrient shortages. As a result of this resource sharing, the ecosystem as a whole is more resilient allowing plants to sustain one another and flourish in harsh environments.

Furthermore, the mycorrhizal network facilitates chemical signaling which allows plants to communicate with one another. A plant has the ability to discharge signaling molecules into the fungal network to respond to disease invasion or herbivore attack. Neighboring plants are able to sense the signals and initiate defense systems in preparation of an imminent threat.

The mycorrhizal network is essential for the health and well-being of plants as it serves as a pathway for the exchange of nutrients and communications. Its complex mechanisms emphasize how interrelated or living things are in the natural environment and how crucial symbiosis is to preserving ecosystem balance and resilience.

However, the forest symbiotic relationships go far beyond the soil and roots. The symbiotic connection between trees and epiphytic plants is a remarkable example of nature's ingenuity where two seemingly dissimilar organisms, trees and epiphytic plants, form a mutually beneficial relationship. The many species of plants known as epiphytic plants-which include ferns, bromeliads, orchids and mosses-have developed special adaptations that enable them to survive in the absence of soil. Instead,they depend on the support of their arboreal for physical anchorage as well as access to moisture and nutrients.

The branches of their arboreal host provide a heaven and food source for these plants which link to them high above the forest floor among a tangle of leaves and branches, their sensitive roots sucking up nutrients and moisture from the surrounding organic matter as well as the atmosphere. The trees also benefit in many ways when epiphytic plants are present. First of all, by drawing moisture and filtering pollutants from the surrounding air these aerial gardeners act as living air purifiers, assisting in the control of microclimate conditions under the canopy.

Epiphytic plants also serve to maintain the general moisture balance of the forest by absorbing water vapor through specialized tissues like trichomes and velamen roots. This helps to lessen the impacts of transpiration and drought. Furthermore, epiphytic plants are essential to the enhancement of biodiversity within the forest canopy and provide a variety of forest organisms with food and habitat.

The dense foliage of epiphytic plants create a veritable oasis of life amidst the leafy expanse, supporting a complex web of ecological interactions that range from insects and spiders to birds and small mammals. Their symbiotic relationship with trees bring about the creation of micro habitats and ecological niches that supports a diverse range of species enhancing the resilience and stability of the forest ecosystem as a whole. Another amazing feature of the symbiotic relationship between trees and epiphytic plants is their capacity to exchange nutrients and organic matter.

As they receive physical support from their arboreal host, epiphytic plants also manufacture organic chemicals and deposit leaf litter which aids in the nutrition cycling within the forest canopy. Epiphytic plants shed leaves, flowers and other organic components as they group and reproduce which build up on the surface of the tree branches and help create a nutrient- rich substrate known as canopy soil.

This organic matrix acts as a rich substrate for the growth of lichens, mosses and other epiphytic plants, fostering the development of a dynamic and self-sustaining ecosystem within the forest canopy. Through the provision of a stable substrate for attachment and growth, trees help epiphytic plants spread and colonize species.This allows the plants to reach new areas and increase their range within the forest ecosystem.

The symbiotic relationship between trees illustrates the complex web of dependency that sustains life in the forest. These two organisms have developed a connection that goes beyond individuality through their delicate dance of mutual benefit, which enhances the general well-being and vigor of the forest ecosystem.

But perhaps the most inspiring example of symbiosis in the forest is the deep relationship between humans and trees which goes beyond simple biological reliance and embraces a rich tapestry of ecological, spiritual and cultural value. Humans have had a close relationship with the forest for millennia because we understand its limitless supply of food, shelter and spiritual support.

Trees have been integral to human awareness throughout history, from the prehistoric customs of indigenous people to the enduring knowledge of mythology and folklore serving as symbols of resilience, strength and connectivity. They have also been regarded as sacred beings throughout history valued for their longevity, wisdom and capacity to sustain life. In gratitude to the forest for its innumerable blessings, humanity has taken on the sacred responsibility of stewardship, realizing that it is our obligation to safeguard and maintain the fragile balance of life that sustains us all.

Over the course of time global civilizations have evolved complex systems of knowledge and practices to conserve and manage Forest resources in a sustainable manner. Some of these systems include the traditional coppicing procedures used in European forests and the indigenous agroforestry techniques used in the Amazon jungle. Through the means of these methods people have developed a profound comprehension of the forest ecosystem and have come to grasp the significance of biodiversity, healthy soil and water conservation for the forest's long-term health and vitality.

The symbiotic relationship between trees and organisms illustrates the complex web of dependency that sustains life in the forest. Every organism has an essential part in determining the health and vitality of the forest ecosystem, from the close relationships that exist between trees and mycorrhizal fungi beneath the soil to the luxurious tapestry canopy and also to us humans. These beautiful relationships remind us of the fundamental connectivity of all living things and the necessity of cherishing and preserving the delicate web of life that supports us all.

CHAPTER 7

TREES AS CULTURAL CANOPIES

Looking at this topic you might wonder "What does trees as cultural canopies mean" or "How do trees act as cultural canopies". Trees as cultural canopies refers to the idea of trees supporting cultural traditions, identities and collective memories by serving as metaphorical and symbolic shelters. In other words the same way a tree's canopy provides shade and protection, trees and forest also serve as a cultural canopy sheltering and influencing human culture, traditions and beliefs, symbolizing the nurturing and sustaining elements of culture within societies.

They represent the interdependence of humans and the natural world, embodying the depth of historical, mythical and spiritual importance across various cultures. As cultural canopies, trees have an important role in preserving and transmitting cultural practices, values and heritage throughout generations.

Imagine yourself walking through the deep forests of antiquity where each tall tree appears to exude a mysterious aura and a sense of profound wisdom resonating with gods and spirits. Not only were trees considered as living things in many ancient societies, They were also highly esteemed as spiritual symbols that were deeply ingrained in mythology and belief systems.

Journeying back to the realms of norse mythology, the powerful Yggdrasil represents the Pinnacle of heavenly order and cosmic superiority. Yggdrasil also known as the world tree is not just a massive oak tree but a sacred emblem that connects the nine realms of existence. Yggdrasil is a symbol of the interlinked nature of all things in norse cosmology.

Traveling east to the ancient regions of India stands the sacred Bodhi tree beckoning to Pilgrims and seekers alike. The historical Buddha Siddhartha Gautama is said to have reached enlightenment beneath its verdant canopy. This revered fig tree often called the Bodhi tree is a living example of spiritual awakening, having inspired countless numbers of followers to pursue enlightenment and inner serenity.

The ancient celts also had mystical traditions,they treated sacred groves with the deepest respect. These enchanting forests were thought to be the home of gods and spirits, where ceremonies were performed and knowledge was passed along.The celts sought comfort and a conduit to the divine among these sacred groves, encouraging a profound respect for the natural environment.

Trees appear as more than just plants in each of these cultural narratives; they become living representations of transcendence that encapsulate the mysteries of life and the interdependence of all living things. From the norse realms to the banks of the Ganges and the misty forests of Celtic land, Trees are like spiritual conduits taking humanity on a voyage of self-discovery and cosmic understanding. Let us keep in mind the profound knowledge encapsulated in the rustling leaves and gnarled branches of the tree as you consider this age old giants.

Trees have also had a profound influence on arts and literature. Authors, poets and artists have all found inspiration in the appeal of trees. Trees as a powerful influence to culture are symbols of life resiliency and beauty and have been woven throughout human creation from William Shakespeare's reflections to Vincent van Gogh's vivid canvas, imagine being taken in time to the Elizabethan, where Shakespeare's words continue to resonate throughout history.

There are also the sun-dappled province landscapes where the vivid colors of the countryside provided Vincent Van Gogh with inspiration and comfort. Vincent van Gogh painted the trees in all their majestic majesty capturing their essence with strong brush strokes and an unmatched mastery of color, each canvas pulsating with the vibrancy and energy of nature beckoning us to immerse ourselves in the beauty of the surrounding environment

However, the exploration of artistic expression by trees goes deeper into the literary canon, where poets and authors have created compelling poetry and prose that draws inspiration from the majestic beauty of trees. Trees have always been associated with mystery, change and renewal weaving their way into the very fabric of storytelling itself.

As we consider the great influence trees have had on art and literature, it is important not to forget the ageless wisdom encapsulated in their silent presence. Trees serve as constant reminders of our intimate connection to nature and its eternal power.

Finally, delving into the bustling landscapes of urban environments, in the middle of the concrete jungle stands the trees providing shade and beauty but most importantly acting as a vital conduit for community connection and preserving cultural traditions. Imagine taking a leisurely stroll along a street surrounded with trees in the middle of the city, the sound of rustling leaves providing a peaceful contrast to the daily bustle. It's cool air against your face whispering stories of resilience and renewal serving as a gentle reminder that nature's love is always around even in the middle of an urban mess.

Take a Stroll through a city park and take a look at the tall trees reaching high into the sky to provide shade from the scorching sun. Here among the fragrant flowers and verdant foliage, friends get together for leisurely walks, families have picnics and kids play in the shade of the leaves.

Trees in urban environments are more than just greenery, they are dynamic tributes to the history and culture of the area. Navigating through the Urban landscape, it is important we appreciate the various ways that trees improve our lives and fortify our sense of community.

Trees are the lifeblood of our culture, sustaining body, mind and soul with their timeless beauty and enduring presence. So next time you see a tree take a moment to acknowledge and appreciate it.

CHAPTER 8

TREE CARE: ARBORICULTURE

Humans and trees are comparable in several ways, both in terms of requirements and the advantages offered to the environment.Trees need to be properly maintained in order to flourish and stay healthy, much like humans. For proper growth, they require sunlight,water, nutrients and space.

Trees depend on us for proper maintenance and care just as we depend on them for a variety of supplies and benefits.Trees provide us with vital ecological,economic and aesthetic benefits and we can guarantee that they continue to flourish by giving them regular care.

Arboriculture is the study and art of maintaining and caring for trees, shrubs and other perennial woody plants in landscapes, orchards, urban settings and forests. It covers the study and maintenance of individual trees and woody plants to maintain their health and aesthetic appeal. The wonderful art of arboriculture includes tree planting, pruning, managing pests and diseases and evaluating tree risks

Within the realm of arboriculture, the intricate dance between human stewardship and nature's grace unveils. Each tree has a narrative to tell, and every arborist becomes the devoted storyteller of that story. A harmonious blend of expertise, care and respect.

Arboriculture isn't just about pruning branches and plant saplings, it is an art form requiring understanding, patience and a strong connection to the soil, it's about understanding disease symptoms, When to prune and when to let nature take its course. It is the right balance between getting involved and letting things happen naturally.

As you learn more about arboriculture, You'll come to the understanding that trees are not just silent spectators of the world but also its heartbeat, they stabilize the ground beneath our feet, offer refuge to innumerable species and purify the air we breathe.

We have an obligation to protect them since they are the silent guardians of our planet. However maintaining trees is not always easy, it calls for commitment, knowledge, and an openness to taking lessons from both achievements and setbacks. Every tree has different difficulties, from fending off pests to enduring storms, but we can support their growth if we have the correct information and resources. Seeing a tree you've been caring for grows is one of the most satisfying parts of arboriculture.

A tree's strength and vitality return when you cut away deadwood and tend to its roots. It serves as evidence of the effectiveness of human intervention and the resilience of nature. However, the capacity of arboriculture to unite us with something bigger than ourselves may be its ultimate beauty.

Trees serve as a constant reminder of our place in the natural order of things in a world where chaos and disconnection are commonplace. They impart to us values such as humility, patience, and the significance of preserving the environment.

Taking care of our trees is more than just a chore; it's a duty that improves the environment's health and aesthetic appeal. Taking good care of your trees guarantees their life and vitality, whether you're looking after a single tree in your backyard or overseeing an entire forest.

Watering is essential to tree care, especially for newly planted trees. Trees need regular watering during this crucial establishment phase in order to promote strong root development and general vigor. However, there is no one-size-fits-all method when it comes to watering; instead, it is influenced by a variety of elements, including the kind of soil, the current climate, and the particular requirements of the tree species in issue.

Determining the frequency and amount of irrigation requires an understanding of the type of soil. Loam and clay soils, which hold moisture effectively, may need less frequent watering than sandy soils, which dry out quickly and require more frequent irrigation.

Additionally, oversaturation, which can suffocate roots and cause rot, can be avoided by checking the moisture content of the soil before watering. The climate affects when trees should be watered. Trees may need more regular watering to compensate for moisture loss in areas that are vulnerable to drought or protracted dry periods. On the other hand, to avoid waterlogging and fungal problems, watering frequency may be decreased in regions with high humidity or regular rainfall. The type of tree being grown should also be considered when watering.

Certain trees—such as bald cypresses or willows—do better in damp environments and could need more frequent watering, whereas other trees-such as cactus or palms that have evolved to the desert are more drought-tolerant and require less frequent watering. Finding out the particular needs of the tree species guarantees specialized treatment that encourages the best possible development and health.

During the actual watering procedure, it is advised to use a gradual, deep watering technique. Because of this, water is able to permeate the soil deeply, which promotes roots to grow downward in search of nutrients and moisture. Frequently shallow watering plants encourage shallow root systems that are vulnerable to drought stress; in contrast, thorough but infrequent watering sessions promote stronger, more durable roots.

Watering should preferably take place once or twice a week during dry months, depending on the requirements of the tree and the surrounding, ensuring that the water gets to the tree's root zone is imperative. This promotes root stability and growth, securing the tree firmly in the ground and strengthening its resistance to external stresses like drought and wind.

Mulching is another important practice in tree care as it conserves moisture, minimizes weed growth and regulates soil temperature. Organic mulching is the use of organic materials such as wood chips or shredded bark, which are particularly noteworthy among the possibilities available because of their capacity to improve soil health and sustain tree growth in the long run.

By slowly breaking down and releasing vital nutrients that support a healthy ecosystem below the surface and nourish tree roots, these organic mulches act as a nutritional powerhouse for the soil. Driven by a complex community of fungus, insects, and microbes, the decomposition of organic mulch is an interesting process. The mulch changes as it decomposes, releasing nutrients and organic stuff into the soil. It also acts as a sponge by keeping moisture in the soil and preventing erosion while at the same time improving soil structure.

Furthermore, the microbial activity induced by decomposing mulch enhances soil fertility and nutrient cycling, fostering an atmosphere that is favorable for the healthy development of roots and general tree vigor.To optimize the benefits and avoid any potential negatives, best techniques must be followed while placing mulch around the base of the tree.

Establishing a "mulch-free zone," or space between the trunk and the mulch, helps keep moisture from building up against the tree's bark, which can cause rot and fungal diseases. Additionally, this area deters pests like rodents from building nests close to the base of the tree, lowering the possibility of harm to the trunk and roots.

Moreover, the mulch layer's efficiency is greatly influenced by its depth. Ideally, a covering of organic mulch should be placed between two and four inches deep, offering sufficient coverage without choking the tree roots or the soil. An excessively thick layer of mulch can act as a barrier, preventing gas exchange and water infiltration, which can cause root asphyxia and other moisture-related problems.

In addition to improving the soil around the tree, organic mulch acts as a natural weed suppressant, lowering competition for water and nutrients and lowering the need for herbicides. Renewing mulch as it breaks down on a regular basis guarantees a steady supply of nutrients and maintains ideal soil conditions.

Mulch helps keep the area surrounding the base of the tree neat and weed-free, improving the tree's aesthetic appeal and requiring less maintenance. It does this by forming a barrier that blocks sunlight and prevents weed germination.

Pruning is a crucial part of caring for trees; it's sometimes compared to an art form since it strikes a delicate balance between aesthetic appeal and functional health. It is a preventative approach that includes a variety of methods, such as strategic canopy shaping and precise branch removal with the ultimate goal of improving sunlight penetration, ventilation, and tree structure.

Primarily, pruning is an essential method for preserving the health of trees by eliminating unhealthy, diseased, or dead branches. If neglected, these damaged branches not only diminish the tree's aesthetic appeal but also run the risk of failing structurally and spreading disease.

Arborists can remove these troublesome branches carefully by focused pruning, thereby enhancing the general vitality of the tree and minimizing the probability of future issues. Furthermore, pruning is essential for forming the canopy of the tree and maximizing its form and structure for better appearance and use. Pruning improves airflow inside the tree by thinning branches selectively and lowering canopy density, this lowers the danger of fungal infections and increases overall tree vigor.

Furthermore, deliberate canopy sculpting enhances the amount of sunlight that reaches the tree's lower branches, guaranteeing that they receive enough light for photosynthesis and encouraging the tree's overall health. When it comes to pruning, timing is everything. Generally speaking, the best time to prune a tree is during its dormant season. When a tree is pruned during dormancy, it experiences less stress because it isn't actively focusing its energy on defense or growth.

Additionally, because pathogens are less active during this time and there is a lower chance of infection at pruning sites, dormant pruning lowers the danger of disease transmission.

The use of appropriate pruning methods and instruments is very crucial in order to guarantee the best outcomes and reduce tree stress. Pruning saws, loppers, and hand pruners are examples of clean, sharp pruning instruments that are necessary to make accurate cuts without causing unwanted damages on surrounding tissues.

Furthermore, cutting at the right angle—just outside the bark ridge or branch collar—speeds up recovery and lowers the chance of disease invasion. Pruning is more successful when tools are maintained properly through routine disinfection and sharpening, which lowers the chance of introducing pathogens.

Pruning improves airflow and sunlight penetration, lowers the danger of disease spread and structural failure, and increases overall tree vitality. Pruning when carefully done prolongs the life and beauty of trees, guaranteeing that they will be beautiful for many years to come.

Proactive tree care revolves around routine inspection, which guarantees early detection and timely treatment of disease or pest infestations. This careful maintenance not only keeps your trees healthy and vibrant, but it also keeps small problems from growing into bigger ones that could endanger the tree's general health. Let's examine the significance of routine inspections in more detail, as well as what to look for and what to do when any problems are discovered.

Regular inspections entail methodically looking over the tree's leaves, branches, bark, and roots to spot any abnormalities or indications of distress. Early problem discovery is essential because it enables prompt intervention, which is frequently easier and more successful than treating disease or insect infestations at advanced stages.

Unusual leaf discoloration is one of the earliest signs of problems with the health of the tree. Healthy leaves usually have a species-specific color that is constant, so if you see leaves becoming brown, yellow, or displaying streaks and patches, there may be an issue,for example, yellowing leaves may be a sign of overwatering, nutrient shortages or root problems while spots could be as a result of root damage or fungal infestation.

Another important symptom to look out for during your inspections is wilting. Wilting leaves especially when there is enough water available can be a sign of vascular diseases like verticillium wilt, pest infestations like those brought on by borers or aphids, or root difficulties. By keeping an eye on things consistently, you can track changes over time and link symptoms to potential causes. Unusual development patterns are further warning signs of possible problems.

Keep an eye out for odd growths on branches and trunks, such as galls or swellings, which may be a result of fungi, bacteria, or insects. Furthermore, malformed leaves, stunted development, or branch dieback may indicate underlying health problems. For instance, branch dieback may indicate the presence of canker infections or root rot, both of which need to be treated right away.

Examining the bark of the tree for indications of problems is an important part of tree inspections. Bark should be solid and undamaged; any peeling, splitting, or holes may be signs of a number of issues, while fissures may be the consequence of physical deterioration, bacterial wetwood diseases,or freeze-thaw cycles,holes may indicate digging insects.

Mushrooms growing at the base of trees or other fungi producing fruiting bodies can be indicators of root rot or decay within the tree's structure. Examining the tree's roots and the vicinity around its base are equally crucial. Keep an eye out for any indications of girdling roots, which can choke a tree by encircling its trunk.

An inspection might also reveal typical problems like physical damage to roots, poor drainage, and compacted soil. It is strongly advised that you visit a certified arborist as soon as you suspect any issues. Professionals with training in tree health diagnosis and treatment recommendation formulation are known as arborists. They can carry out further in-depth assessments, such as soil testing, pest identification, and disease diagnosis, to create a comprehensive care plan customized to your tree's unique requirements.

Depending on the problem, arborists can offer a wide range of treatment solutions, they may suggest chemical or cultural methods to curb pest infestation. Fungicides, trimming of afflicted areas and enhancing soil health with organic amendments and aeration are some possible treatments for illnesses.

To stabilize trees whose structural integrity has been damaged, it may occasionally be essential to provide structural support using bracing and cabling. In order to discover pest infestations and illnesses early on and effectively control them, routine inspections are an essential part of tree maintenance. You may immediately address problems with your trees before they worsen by keeping an eye out for symptoms of distress, such as strange leaf discolouration, wilting, aberrant growth, and bark damage.

By speaking with a certified arborist, you are confident that you'll receive professional advice on diagnosis and treatment, preserving the longevity and aesthetic appeal of your trees. Therefore, pay closer attention to your trees the next time you stroll among them; they may be attempting to tell you something important.

Lastly but not the least is Fertilization, Promoting the health of trees requires regular fertilization, especially for those planted in soils poor in nutrients. In contrast to trees found in natural woods, which usually obtain their nutrients from the decaying organic waste around them, trees found in urban or groomed settings frequently need extra fertilizer to survive. Let's examine the complex process of fertilizing trees, from determining the needs of the soil to using fertilizers wisely and responsibly.

Doing a soil test is the first step in fertilizing trees. Doing this can give you a wealth of information about the nutrients in your soil. Tests on soil determine the concentrations of secondary nutrients and micronutrients including calcium, magnesium, and iron in addition to basic nutrients like nitrogen (N), phosphorus (P), and potassium (K).

These tests evaluate the pH of the soil, which affects nutrient availability. It is possible to precisely address any short falls in your fertilization strategy by knowing the unique nutrient profile of your soil.The process of choosing the right fertilizer gets considerably simpler once you have the results of the soil test. Fertilizers are available in a variety of formulas, each tailored to meet specific nutrient requirements.

A balanced fertilizer, such as 10-10-10, which has an equal N-P-K ratio, offers a wide range of nutrients. On the other hand, you may choose to use a specialty fertilizer, such as one strong in phosphorus to assist root development and blooming or one high in nitrogen to encourage foliage growth. If your soil test results reveal a particular shortage.For maximum effect, fertilizers must be applied at the right time. For the most part, trees should be fertilized in the spring and fall.

Spring fertilization helps the plants grow rapidly as they break dormancy and begin producing new leaves and shoots while on the other hand, fall fertilization helps trees recover from the strains of the growing season and gets them ready for winter. Selecting the appropriate type of fertilizer is not as crucial as applying it correctly.

Overfertilization can cause nutrient runoff, which damages aquatic habitats and contaminates streams. Moreover, it may result in a buildup of salt in the soil, which can cause root burn and other symptoms of plant stress. Always use the prescribed application rates and techniques to avoid these problems.There are various ways to fertilize trees, and each works well in a particular situation, some are;

Surface Application:Applying granular fertilizer uniformly to the soil's surface along the tree's drip line—where the majority of feeder roots are found—is known as surface application. After application, watering the region aids in the dissolution of the granules and carries the nutrients into the root zone.

Soil Injection:This entails the injection of liquid fertilizer directly into the soil at different points around the tree's root zone with the use of specialized equipment. Nutrients will reach the root system more rapidly and effectively with this strategy.

Foliar feeding;This entails sprinkling the leaves of the tree with a diluted liquid fertilizer. For micronutrients that are easily absorbed by the leaf, this technique can offer a rapid nutrient boost.

Fertilizers with slow release: Using slow-release formulations, which release nutrients over a longer time period gradually, improves the long-term health of trees by lowering the chance of overfertilization and supplying a consistent supply of nutrients. To further enhance nutrient availability, adding organic matter to the soil can help tremendously.

In addition to providing necessary nutrients, organic materials like compost, well-rotted manure, and leaf mold also strengthen soil structure, retain more water and encourage healthy microbial activity. Fertilizer also helps trees cope with a range of environmental challenges.

Trees in urban areas are usually associated with issues including pollution, congested soil, and restricted root area and frequent fertilization ensures that these trees receive the nutrients they need to continue growing strongly and resiliently even in restricted root areas.

Frequent fertilization ensures that these trees receive the nutrients they need to continue growing strongly and resiliently, which helps to alleviate these pressures.

Additionally, fertilization is essential for maintaining recently planted trees. As their root systems establish themselves in a new site, young trees frequently go through a period of adjustment known as transplant shock. Supplying the appropriate and necessary nutrients at this crucial stage can promote root development and hasten its establishment.

Fertilization is an essential aspect of thorough tree care, especially for trees growing in soils lacking in nutrients. You can make sure that your trees get the nutrients they require to flourish by testing the soil, choosing the right fertilizers, and applying them when and how they should.

In addition to encouraging strong development and vivid foliage, proper fertilization also strengthens the tree's resistance to environmental challenges, preserving its health and beauty for many years to come. The next time you consider your trees, keep in mind that providing them with little nutrients can help them grow into mature, magnificent trees.

Taking the tree's surroundings into account is another aspect of proper tree maintenance. Ample room for root propagation should be ensured by staying away from surrounding structures or compacted soil that might impede growth.

Finally, plant native species and create habitat for wildlife and beneficial insects to increase biodiversity around trees. Resilience against environmental shocks is fostered by healthy ecosystems supporting healthy plants.

Taking good care of trees involves a mix of dedication, understanding, and reverence for the natural world. For our trees to flourish we have to take good care of them and this can be done by carefully following the steps listed above , by doing so we can nurture trees that will thrive for generations to come.

CONCLUSION

HONORING THE WISDOM OF TREES

Imagine yourself standing in a calm woodland,the sunlight gleaming above you. The sound of a trickling stream in the distance and the soothing chirping of birds harmonized with the delicate rustling of leaves overhead. Crisp and cold, the air is scented with the earthy notes of moist soil, pine needles, and wildflowers. This location is more than simply a serene getaway; it's a living example of the harmony of nature, where the age-old wisdom of the trees drifts through the branches.

You have a strong sense of connectedness to the surrounding natural environment while you stand there. Trees, with their enormous roots that securely bind them to the ground, and their towering canopies have been silent observers of time's passage. These magnificent giants have withstood innumerable seasons, storms, droughts, and changes in the terrain.

Numerous lessons about resiliency, community, and balance may be learned just from their presence. Trees are resilient; they adjust to their surroundings. Some stand hard and sturdy, their deep roots and thick bark offering stability and protection, while others bend beautifully in the breeze, their suppleness keeping them from breaking. Every tree conveys a tale of overcoming obstacles to flourish and survive.

The complex subterranean networks that link trees to one other are examples of community. By means of their roots and mutualistic associations with fungus, trees exchange information, exchange nutrients, and facilitate the growth of one another. This intricate network of relationships highlights the significance of cooperation and mutual aid, showing the interconnectivity of life within the forest.

Trees offer food and shelter to many species and keep a careful balance between the demands of various species and the wellbeing of the ecosystem. The health of the entire forest community is guaranteed by the presence of trees. To really honor the wisdom of trees, we must do more than just admire their majesty and beauty; we must also investigate their complex lives and acknowledge the deep lessons they may provide.

We need to understand that trees are essential components of a complex and interconnected ecosystem, not just isolated individual units. Through examining their patterns of development, means of survival, and social interactions, we may learn more about how to coexist peacefully and sustainably in our own community.

We can honor the wisdom of trees in so many ways such as;

1.Spending time with trees: Spend time in a forest or nature reserve, hug a tree, or just sit at its base. Perceive the energy of the forest, pay attention to the sounds of the trees, and let yourself become one with nature.

2. Studying tree mythology and symbolism: Examine the spiritual and cultural meanings of trees in various

traditions and cultures. Discover the mythology and symbolism connected to different types of trees.

3. Planting a tree: Honoring the wisdom of trees and contributing to the natural world can be done by planting a tree. Select a local tree species and plant it in an environment that will support its growth.

4. Practicing tree meditation: This technique entails concentrating on a tree, examining its form, texture, and motion, and allowing yourself to become mindful and in the moment.

5. Making an art inspired by trees: Use writing, music, or art to convey how much you value trees. Make an artwork that captures the grace and knowledge of trees.

6. Encouraging reforestation: Give your support to groups that plant trees and rebuild forests. By contributing, you can honor the wisdom of trees and safeguard the environment.

7. Honoring Arbor Day: Honoring the value of trees, Arbor Day is a holiday. Take part in a nearby Arbor Day celebration, plant a tree, or attend a tree-planting ceremony.

8. Acquiring knowledge about conservation and tree care: Acquire knowledge about the significance of conservation and tree care. Learn how to take good care of your trees and contribute to the efforts being made to save and maintain tree species.

9. Making a tree altar: Establish a hallowed area in your house or garden to pay homage to the knowledge that trees possess. In a special location, plant a small tree or branch, and surround it with items that symbolize your relationship to the natural world.

10. Developing appreciation: Every day, take a moment to express your gratitude for the knowledge that trees and the natural world have to offer. Consider the ways that trees have helped and inspired you.

Respecting the wisdom of trees is a complex process that includes caring for the environment, appreciating biodiversity, taking lessons from nature's resilience, building community, and improving our general well-being. Trees are incredibly beneficial and teach us important lessons about the delicate balance of life and our place in it.

We guarantee a world that is healthier, more resilient, and harmonious for present and future generations by appreciating and preserving trees. Let's listen to the trees' unspoken wisdom as we stroll among them and allow it to lead us to a greater comprehension and appreciation of the natural world.

COMMON TERMS OF TREES

Bark: Woody plants' outermost stem and root layers. It protects the tree from physical damage and disease.

Bole: Refers to the tree's trunk.

Cambium: A layer of cells between the wood and the bark that generates new wood and bark.

Canopy: The upper layer of trees in a forest is made up of the tallest trees' leaves and branches.

Conifer: Pines and firs are examples of trees that produce cones and needle-like or scale-like leaves while remaining mostly evergreen.

Deciduous: Refers to trees or shrubs that lose their leaves seasonally, typically in autumn.

Dendrochronology: The scientific dating method that uses tree ring patterns to determine age.

Evergreen: Refers to a tree with green leaves year-round.

The leaf: A part of the tree, typically flat and green, primarily responsible for photosynthesis

Abscission: Refers to the process of trees shedding their leaves, flowers, or fruit, which is often caused by seasonal changes.

Adaptation: A characteristic that allows a tree to survive and reproduce in its environment, such as needle-like leaves in conifers that reduce water loss.

Allee effect: A phenomenon in ecology in which the size or density of tree populations influences the growth rate and survival of individual trees, which is commonly observed in isolated trees or small groves.

Angiosperm: A tree that produces flowers and seeds in the form of fruit, e.g, maples and oaks

Annual ring: A ring in a tree trunk's cross section that represents one year of growth and is made up of springwood and summerwood layers.

Bark Beetle: An insect that burrows underground in tree barks, causing death and destruction to trees.

Base Area: A measurement of a tree trunk's cross-sectional area at breast height that is used in forestry to estimate the volume of timber in the stand.

Biome: A large community of plants and animals that live in a specific region defined by its climate and dominant vegetation, such as a temperate forest.

Boreal Forest: Coniferous trees, such as pines and spruces, characterize this forest biome, which can be found in colder northern regions.

Buttress Root: In tropical forests, large roots on all the sides of shallowly rooted trees, which provide stability and support.

Canker: A disease that causes sunken, dead areas on trees' bark, branches, or twigs.

Catkin: A slim, cylindrical flower cluster found in trees such as willows and birches that is frequently pollinated by the wind.

Phloem: The vascular tissue in trees that transports sugars and other metabolic products downward from the leaves.

Photosynthesis: The process by which green plants use sunlight to synthesize foods using chlorophyll in their leaves, while producing oxygen as a byproduct.

Sap: The fluid that circulates in a plant's vascular system and is primarily made up of water with dissolved sugars and mineral salts.

Seeds: The reproductive parts of trees that can grow into new trees. Seeds are typically found inside a fruit or cone.

Shrubs: Woody plants that are smaller than trees and have multiple stems.

Silviculture: The practice of managing the growth, composition, health, and quality of forests to meet a variety of needs and values.

Stomata: Microscopic pores on the leaves' surface that allow for gas exchange.

Transpiration: The process by which moisture is transported through plants from roots to small pores on the underside of leaves, where it is converted to vapor and released into the atmosphere.

Understory: A layer of vegetation beneath a forest's main canopy, which includes shrubs and young trees.

Xylem: The vascular tissue in trees that transports water and dissolved nutrients up from the roots to the rest of the tree.

Dormancy: A season, usually brought on by cold weather, in which a tree's growth and metabolic processes slow down or cease.

Epiphyte: A plant that grows on another plant (such as a tree) but is not parasitic; common in tropical forests.

Forest floor: Bottom layer of the forest composed of soil, leaf litter, and decomposing organic matter.

Girdling: The removal of a strip of bark around a tree's circumference, which can kill the tree by disrupting the flow of nutrients.

Heartwood: The dense interior of a tree trunk that provides structural support and fights decay.

Hydraulic Lift: A process where deep-rooted trees transport water from deeper soil layers to the surface, benefiting nearby vegetation.

Leaf litter: Dead and decaying leaves that fall into the forest providing organisms with a place to live and improving soil fertility.

Mast year: When trees produce an excessive amount of seeds,this occur irregularly.

Nurse's Log: A fallen tree trunk that decays and provides a fertile environment for new seedlings to grow.

Phenology: The investigation of the timing of seasonal events in trees, such as leafing, flowering, and fruiting.

Pioneer Species:The first trees to colonize a disturbed or newly formed area, thereby starting ecological succession.

Pollarding: This is a tree management technique in which upper branches are cut back to encourage dense growth of new shoots.

Resin: A sticky, viscous substance produced by certain trees commonly used to protect against insects and pathogens.

Riparian Zone: The area between land and a river or stream that is frequently characterized by specific tree and plant species that thrive in wet conditions.

Sapling: A young tree, more than a seedling but not yet attained maturity.

Self-Pruning: A tree's natural shedding of lower branches, often caused by shading and a lack of light.

Snag: A standing dead tree that serves as wildlife habitat and contributes to forest ecology.

Softwood: Usually softer and used in construction and paper making, mostly from coniferous trees.

Suckers: Asexual shoots that grow from a tree's roots or base.

www.ingramcontent.com/pod-product-compliance
Lightning Source LLC
Chambersburg PA
CBHW050824250726
48653CB00006B/2411

* 9 7 9 8 3 2 7 1 4 8 5 3 6 *